not a guide to

Glasgow

Bruce Durie

First published 2012

The History Press
The Mill, Brimscombe Port
Stroud, Gloucestershire, GL5 2QG
www.thehistorypress.co.uk

British Library Cataloguing in Publication Data.
A catalogue record for this book is available from the British Library.

ISBN 978 0 7524 6634 7

Typesetting and origination by The History Press
Printed in Great Britain

Coat of Arms

The city's arms (here on the Concert Hall) show
St Mungo, patron saint and first Bishop of Glasgow, plus
events connected with his life and work.

*

He is said to have preached a sermon with the words
'Lord, Let Glasgow flourish by the preaching of the word
and the praising of thy name.' This was later abbreviated
to 'Let Glasgow Flourish' and adopted as the city's motto.

*

The tree is for a frozen branch which Mungo lit by blowing
on it and used to re-kindle the fire at Culross monastery in
Fife. The bird is a robin he brought back to life. The fish and
ring refer to a love token given away by Langueth, wife of
King Ridderch of Strathclyde, which Mungo predicted would
be found in a salmon from the Clyde. The bell is the one he
brought back from Rome.

Contents

Glasgow

With a cathedral and a university, Glasgow has come a long way from a medieval fishing village. In the process, it has changed its status from western backwater to Scotland's largest and most stylish city, by way of slaves, sugar and tobacco, shipbuilding and heavy engineering, Second City of Empire, the 'No Mean City' epithet that accompanied the Depression, the tenement clearances and rebirth of the 1960s and '70s and the growing sense of self-worth that blossomed at the turn of the twentieth and twenty-first centuries.

It was a place of slums and grandeur, of razor gangs and poets, of sectarian violence and cultural assimilation. The Glaswegians have welcomed (and occasionally harassed) Irish, Jewish, Italian, Polish, Asian, Chinese and even English settlers. It is now one of the most ethnically diverse yet integrated and culturally vibrant cities in Britain.

Glasgow, facing westwards with a view to the wider world and its back firmly set against anything coming from Edinburgh, is a city that invites (and invents) superlatives – 'best' this, 'first' that, 'longest' the other. The denizens are funny, warm and hardworking but also have a reputation for being morose or feckless. The predominant religion is football.

It has more comedians than Liverpool, more engineers than Birmingham, better education than Oxford, fabulous Georgian and Victorian architecture and excellent Italian ice cream.

Cultural Orientation

On chips – Salt 'n' vinegar (instead of salt 'n' sauce) betrays a leaning towards Edinburgh-ish behaviour and invites a good kicking.

Greggs – Walk around New York and everyone is carrying a hold-all from Saks 5th Avenue. In Glasgow, it's a paper bag from the famous chain of bakers, probably holding a sausage roll or twelve mini-donuts.

Irn-Bru – To the bewilderment and inchoate fury of Coca-Cola, Pepsi and the other global fizzy-pop brands, the national beverage is Irn-Bru, taken with all known spirits (yes, even whisky) and occasionally on its own. Just to confuse matters, all flavoured carbonated drinks are known collectively as 'ginger', whether they contain ginger or not.

The Origin of the Name

It is often said that St Mungo called his community's new home *Glasgu*, the 'dear green place', but it is more likely to have come from the older British *glas cau* meaning 'green hollow' or possibly 'grey hollow' – or even 'dear family'. The Gaelic version *Glasgu* appears for the first time in about 1116. The settlement probably had an earlier name, *Cathures*.

Where is it?
55° 52' N, 4° 15' W

OS grid reference: NS590655

Time zone: UTC/GMT

The Greater Glasgow metropolitan area occupies more than 100 square miles, but the central area of the city is compact. Almost all visitor activity is concentrated in the city centre and the West End.

Geotopography

Go to any city in the world (except possibly in the Netherlands) and the natives will tell you that it is built on seven hills. But Glasgow really is – except they are called 'drumlins' – from Golf Hill (now the Necropolis), Drumchattan and what was Bell's Park in the east to Blythswood, Garnethill and Woodside in the west, plus Gilmorehill (site of Glasgow University since 1870).

Glasgow has 27 miles of motorway, 1,068 miles of public roads and 6.5 miles of subway.

Glasgow's infrastructure is aging and struggles to meet the needs of the city's economy (especially water and sewerage). However, new road works go on constantly – leading to the local belief that Glasgow City Council owns one road hole and keeps moving it around.

The city is a major hub for Scottish transport – but there is still no train to Glasgow International airport.

Distance From...

Place	Miles	Km
Athens, Greece	1,783	2,869
Brussels, Belgium	497	800
Campbell Island, NZ (the furthest away place you can actually get to (52° 30' S, 169° 5' E)	12,074	19,430
Canberra, Australia	10,538	16,959
Centre of the Earth	3,976	6,399
Dublin, Ireland	192	310
Edinburgh, Scotland	As far as possible!	
Glasgow Island, Greenland	1,155	1,859
Glasgow Island, Marlborough, NZ	11,457	18,434
Glasgow, Delaware, USA (pop. 13,000)	3,337	5,370
Glasgow, Guyana	4,492	7,229
Glasgow, Illinois, USA (pop. 161)	3,884	6,252
Glasgow, Jamaica	4,506	7,251
Glasgow, Kentucky, USA (pop. 14,200)	3,848	6,193
Glasgow, Missouri, USA (pop. 1,189)	3,986	6,414
Glasgow, Montana, USA (pop. 3,250)	3,973	6,395
Glasgow, Nickerie, Suriname	4,481	7,212
Glasgow, Pennsylvania, USA (pop. 63)	3,465	5,577
Glasgow, Virginia, USA (pop. 1,046)	3,574	5,752
Glasgow, West Virginia, USA (pop. 783)	3,619	5,825
New Glasgow, Nova Scotia, Canada (pop. 9,500)	2,565	4,128

Twin Towns

Town twinning started after the Second World War to foster mutual understanding between cities and countries, initially in Europe.

Glasgow is twinned with Dalian, China; Havana, Cuba (leading to a jointly funded film celebrating the fiftieth anniversary of the Cuban Revolution); Lahore, Pakistan; Nuremberg, Germany; Rostoy on Don, Russia; and Turin, Italy.

The most recent additions to Glasgow's twin cities are Marseilles, in 2006, and Bethlehem, Palestinian Territories. Glasgow and Bethlehem have had a friendship agreement since 1990 and signed a formal town-twinning arrangement in 2007, offering support and solidarity in recognition of 'the special circumstances prevailing in Bethlehem'.

Facts and Figures

Population

Glasgow	2001	2005	2009
Population	578,700	578,800	588,500
Male Population	273,000	276,900	284,700
Female Population	305,700	301,900	303,800
Births	6,645	6,833	7,512
Deaths	7,680	7,072	6,571
Net Migration	-214	2,100	3,575

Demographics (2009)

	Under-16	16-59	60+
Females:	16%	63%	21%
Males:	16%	67%	17%

Roughly equal numbers of over-sixteens are single or married.

Ethnicity

Greater Glasgow has the largest black and minority ethnic (BME) population in Scotland – 5.5 per cent or 48,000 people, which is 39 per cent of the total Scottish BME population.

Some 66 per cent of all BME people in Greater Glasgow are South Asian (19,000, including 12,000 people of Pakistani origin) and about 13 per cent (4,000) are Chinese.

Historical Demography

Is Glasgow getting smaller or bigger? It depends what you mean. The population of Glasgow (the City Council area) was highest in the 1950s at 1,089,000, making Glasgow one of the most densely populated cities in the world. From the 1960s many of the city-centre slums (and, it must be said, some good but dense housing) were cleared and the populace relocated to 'new towns' such as East Kilbride and Cumbernauld. Boundary changes, such as the loss of Cambuslang and Rutherglen to South Lanarkshire in 1996, reduced the area. The current total Greater Glasgow Urban Area is about 400 square miles (1,000 km^2).

Large numbers of **Irish immigrants** settled since the 1840s, chiefly from County Donegal – at one point only New York City had more Irish than Glasgow. The so-called 'Highland Clearances' (which were largely voluntary economic migration) saw much migration from the North and West of Scotland. Both trends also meant a growth of the Catholic population of the city.

Jewish immigrants – mostly from the region covered by parts of Lithuania, Poland and Russia – arrived as a result of persecution and pogroms, and many settled in the Gorbals.

In the late nineteenth and early twentieth centuries, there was an influx of **Lithuanian refugees** and economic migrants, mainly Catholic – some 10,000 were settled in the Glasgow area by the 1950s but are often confused with Polish immigrants.

Italian Scots mainly originated in the provinces of Lucca in north-west Tuscany and Frosinone, between Rome and Naples.

The 1960s and 1970s saw many **Asian-Scots** arriving in Glasgow, mainly to Pollokshields and surrounding areas – estimates give 30,000 from Pakistan, 15,000 from India and 3,000 from Bangladesh, plus Chinese immigrants to the historically Jewish-dominated Garnethill.

Street Names

As late as 1750 there were only thirteen streets in Glasgow:

Bell Street, opened 1710 and named for Sir John Bell, provost, in 1680.

Bridgegate (Briggate), which dates back to 1100. Before the bridge was built it was known as the Fishergate after the incorporated fishermen and fish dealers who built most of it.

Candleriggs, opened in 1724 – there was a candleworks at the north end.

Canon Street, dating from 1360, this street was built on the site of what had been a seminary for training clerics.

Drygate, the oldest street in the city, refers to the Pagan word *dry* indicating a priest or druid – and there was indeed a Druidical place of worship on the site of the present Necropolis, approached by the priests' road or Drygate.

Gallowgate, the street of Gallow Muir beyond the Gallowgate Port near St Mungo's Lane.

High Street, which opened in 1100, led from the Mercat Cross to the highest part of the town but was of no importance until Glasgow University was built on the College Lands.

King Street in the city and **King Street** in Calton were both called New Street until the early 1800s.

Princes Street, which ran between Saltmarket and King Street, dated from 1724, replacing **Gibson's Wynd** (after Walter Gibson, provost in 1688) but has itself now disappeared.

Rottenrow, originally Rattan Raw, has had complete books dedicated to explaining its name, but no one is any the wiser – Glasgow University started off there in 1454 and the University of Strathclyde occupies it now.

Saltmarket, which was **Walcargate** (the place of cloth waulkers or fullers) from 1100, became the market for salt about 1650.

Stockwell Street was the site of a well operated by a wooden stock and of a *buchts* (a feeing or hiring fair).

Trongate was **Saint Thenew's Gate** but changed when the 'tron' (official weighing scale) was placed there.

THOMAS HUTCHESON
DIED 1641

HOSPITAL

Later Street Names

Adelphi Street (early 1800s) was named after the philanthropic Hutcheson brothers, whose statues are on their hospital.

Albany Street in Bridgeton was named after Charlotte Stuart, Duchess of Albany and the daughter of Prince Charlie; she was immortalised by Robert Burns as 'The Bonnie Lass of Albany'. However, she was no Glasgow native but was born in Paris; Charlotte died at Fribourg in Switzerland in 1802.

Argyle Street was originally known as Dumbarton Road, then Wester Gate, then Anderson Walk and finally named after Archibald, Duke of Argyle. This proved prophetic: the Duke died in England, but while en route to his intended burial at Kilmun his body lay in state at Durie's Black Bull Hotel in Argyle street.

Broomielaw, meaning a grassy slope with yellow broom growing on it, had its first quay in 1662.

Byres Road refers to the cow-byres of the clachan (village) of Partick, where cattle would be rested and fed on their way to market. There was an attempt to tidy up the name to Victoria Road, but the sensible Glasgow public rebelled against it.

Drury Street was named by two stage-struck youths who were enamoured of London's Drury Lane Theatre. They put a printed name on the corner building and it stuck, in both senses.

Franklin Street is named after the American statesman, philosopher, scientist and spy Benjamin Franklin.

French Street was originally Papillon Street after Pierre Jacques Papillon, brought from Rouen in France in 1785 to look after a red-dyeing workshop.

George Square, which opened in 1787, was named in honour of King George III and was meant to have his statue in the centre. Occasionally the authorities enclosed the square in railings, but the Glasgow folk always tore them down.

George Street dates from 1792.

Gorbals derives from *garbales*, an old Scots law term for teinds or tithes (a *garb* is a sheaf of wheat, barley, corn etc).

Jamaica Street opened in 1763 at the height of the trade in tobacco, rum, sugar and slaves.

Maryhill was part of the estate of Gairbraid owned by Mary Hill. It's that simple!

Queen Street, previously **Cow Lone**, was built on the property of a man named McCall, an ardent royalist, and thus named for Queen Charlotte when opened in 1777.

Sauchiehall Street was originally *sauchiehaugh*, meaning a *haugh* or water-meadow with *saugh* (willow) trees. No hall at all! It was said that the Glasgow police never arrested anyone here because it was hard to spell – they dragged them to Hope Street instead!

Two Saints – Mother and Son

There are many good ways to start a 'rammy' in a Glasgow pub but one of the most reliable is to point out that both of the city's patron saints came from Fife.

St Thenew (Enoch)

It surprises many that St Enoch was a woman (St Mungo's mother). Thenew, daughter of King Lot of Northumbria, had visions of being a second Virgin Mary. Her father found this a bit strong and put his pregnant daughter to sea in a small boat. This was driven by winds to Culross in Fife, where her son Kentigern was born.

St Mungo

Kentigern's father was Ewan ap Urien, a prince of Strathclyde. He was possibly educated by Saint Serf, who gave him into the care of Semanus, Bishop of Orkney. Semanus found the boy so kind and gentle that he gave him a pet name of his own – Mungo (from the Norwegian *mongah*, meaning friend or dear one). Saint Mungo established the first church in Glasgow.

His statue is at the entrance to the magnificent Kelvingrove Museum, which, contrary to local legend, was not built back-to-front because the architect went away and the builders got the plans upside down: it was designed that way, but the road layout changed.

Historical Timeline

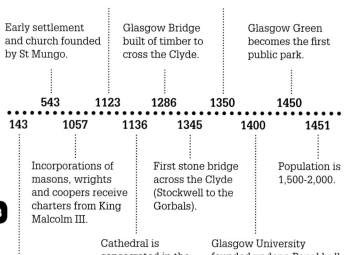

Cathedral is built over
Saint Mungo's grave.

The Black Death
hits Glasgow.

Early settlement
and church founded
by St Mungo.

Glasgow Bridge
built of timber to
cross the Clyde.

Glasgow Green
becomes the first
public park.

543   1123   1286   1350   1450

143   1057   1136   1345   1400   1451

Incorporations of
masons, wrights
and coopers receive
charters from King
Malcolm III.

First stone bridge
across the Clyde
(Stockwell to the
Gorbals).

Population is
1,500-2,000.

Cathedral is
consecrated in the
presence of David I.

Glasgow University
founded under a Papal bull
of Nicholas V, making it the
second oldest in Scotland,
after St Andrews.

Antonine Wall built from
present-day Old Kilpatrick (the
north-eastern end of the Roman
world) to Carron on the Forth,
separated unconquered Caledonia
from the rest of Britain. It was
abandoned after eighty years
in favour of Hadrian's Wall.

Population 5,000-7,500. Glasgow is the fifth largest Scottish burgh before a fire destroys a large part of the town.

Tolbooth Steeple raised at Glasgow Cross.

Plagues ravage Glasgow again.

The Jesuit Father John Ogilvy is hanged for saying Mass.

Glasgow's fourteen Trades are incorporated.

Golf is played on Glasgow Green.

1516-1559   1574 & 1584   1589   1600   1615   1626

1568   1588   1593   1610   1625   1636

Plague hits Paisley and travel from Glasgow is forbidden.

The Bishops are restored in Scotland.

First quay built at Broomielaw.

Battle of Langside. Mary Queen of Scots loses her crown.

Glasgow Presbytery founded in the new reformed Church of Scotland.

Glasgow becomes a Royal Burgh and the university has 120 students.

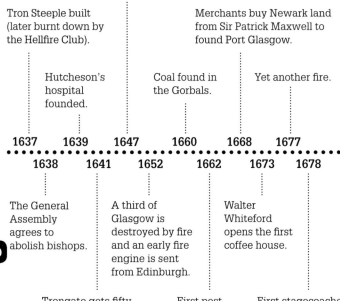

More plague and Glasgow University evacuates to Ayrshire.

Tron Steeple built (later burnt down by the Hellfire Club).

Merchants buy Newark land from Sir Patrick Maxwell to found Port Glasgow.

Hutcheson's hospital founded.

Coal found in the Gorbals.

Yet another fire.

1637   1639   1647   1660   1668   1677

1638   1641   1652   1662   1673   1678

The General Assembly agrees to abolish bishops.

A third of Glasgow is destroyed by fire and an early fire engine is sent from Edinburgh.

Walter Whiteford opens the first coffee house.

Trongate gets fifty new buildings.

First post office opens.

First stagecoaches to Edinburgh.

Population about 12,000 with 450 merchants, 100 trading abroad and 400 students at the university.

The Clyde floods parts of Bridgegate and Saltmarket.

Daniel Defoe calls Glasgow 'the beautifullest little city I have seen in Britain' and 'the cleanest and best-built city in Britain'. Fifty ships sail to America.

Union with England – trade with America is again possible.

Glasgow overtakes Liverpool, Bristol and Whitehaven as a port, largely thanks to the Virginia tobacco trade and slavery.

Clyde deepened beyond The Broomielaw.

1700   1707   1712   1720   1726   1740

1706   1711   1718   1725   1738   1750

Anti-unionists riot. Glasgow is a major focus for smuggling.

First Glasgow ship sails to America. Cotton printing begins.

First shops opened in The Trongate.

200 shops are open. Glasgow ship owners have forty-six vessels, only about 5 per cent of Scottish fleet.

Glasgow occupied by General Wade. Protests and riots against liquor tax.

New Town Hall started near the Tollbooth. Anderston Weavers' Society founded.

Printing starts in the city. The Clyde is dredged to make Glasgow a deep water port and shipbuilding starts, but American Independence destroys the tobacco trade.

Chemical and textile industries start up. Tennants' Brewery opens. Ships of over 30 tons can reach Broomielaw.

The Merchant Banking Co. of Glasgow collapses.

James Watt works as an instrument maker at the university.

Broomielaw jetties built. Trade with America in tobacco, sugar and cotton ensure Glasgow's prosperity.

Trades House built in Glassford Street by Robert Adam, but he dies before finishing it.

1757   1770   1775   1780   1794   1798

1769   1772   1776   1783   1796

James Watt patents the steam engine with an external condenser and the industrial revolution starts.

Adam Smith publishes *The Wealth of Nations* and invents modern economics.

Glasgow Chamber of Commerce is the first modern trade organisation in Britain.

Jamaica Street Bridge opens. Benjamin Franklin oversees the installation of a lightning conductor on the steeple of the university in the High Street.

Anderson's University (later the Royal Technical College and the University of Strathclyde) is founded.

Nelson's column erected on Glasgow Green, Europe's first public park.

Botanic Gardens opened. Market halls built at Candleriggs.

James Beaumont Nielson invents the new hot blast furnace iron-smelting method at Glasgow Gasworks.

The Clyde is 14ft deep and has 200 jetties and wharves. The Glasgow Police Act establishes the first modern police force.

Bell's Comet is Europe's first successful commercial steamship.

Charles Mackintosh produces waterproof garments in his father's chemical works at Dennistoun.

| 1800 | 1806 | 1812 | 1817 | 1823 | 1828 |
| 1799 | 1802 | 1811 | 1813 | 1818 | 1827 | 1831 |

Tobacco and rum trades decline. Riots over bread prices.

Glasgow is now the 'second city of Empire'.

Typhus epidemic. Public gas supply starts.

Argyll Arcade opens.

Glasgow & Garnkirk Railway is the first in Scotland.

The *Charlotte Dundas* – the world's first steam-powered tugboat – pulls two 70-ton barges on the canal.

General Association of Operative Weavers (formed 1809) fails to obtain fair wages.

William Thomson defines the absolute scale of temperature later named after him when he becomes Lord Kelvin. Further cholera epidemic. 'Chartist' riots.

Glasgow Scotland's largest city, with almost 20 per cent of residents Irish-born

Cholera outbreak in the city.

Clydesdale Bank opens.

Botanic Gardens reopen in the growing West End. Glasgow to Edinburgh Railway opens.

St Vincent Street church designed by Alexander 'Greek' Thomson.

Jamaica Street Bridge is widened.

1832 1836 1838 1842 1848 1851 1858

1834 1837 1841 1845 1850 1853 1860

Leaders of cotton-spinners strike transported to Australia.

Glasgow City Halls built.

The new Loch Katrine reservoir gives Glasgow the purest water in Britain.

Prestwick hosts the first British Open Golf Championship.

Kirkman Finlay (1772-1842) brings the first shipment of tea from India to Glasgow direct.

First Omnibus runs between Anderston and Bridgeton. The Great Famine drives the start of immigration from Ireland.

James McCulloch leaves Glasgow for Australia and later becomes Prime Minister of Victoria (1863-68).

Glasgow University moves to its present site at Gilmorehill. First Sanitary Inspector appointed.

Glasgow Underground opens, third after London and Budapest

Joseph Lister introduces antiseptic surgery with carbolic acid.

The City Chambers are built to a design by William Young.

Glasgow's manufacturing dominates Scottish industry.

Glasgow Rangers Football Club founded.

1860-1865   1866-1870   1873   1883   1896   1900

1866   1872   1876   1888   1899

The first Municipal Hospital opens (the Fever Hospital).

First tramway route opens between St George's Cross and Eglinton Toll. Glasgow School Board formed.

Glasgow's *Evening Times* begins publishing. Thomas Lipton opens his first tea, coffee and grocery shop, advertising it on pigs driven through the city

The International Exhibition opens at Kelvingrove Park. Celtic Football Club founded.

Jamaica Street Bridge re-widened.

Population 762,000. The International Exhibition is held at Kelvingrove and the Glasgow Museum and Art Gallery opens.

Glasgow-born Arthur Whitten Brown becomes first to cross the Atlantic by air with John Alcock, eight days ahead of Lindbergh.

The Mitchell Library opens and becomes the largest municipal reference library in Europe.

Population peaks at just over 1 million – second to London.

Charles Rennie Mackintosh dies.

1901   1911   1919   1928   1931

1902   1913   1927   1929   1935

Hampden Park opens for Queen's Park Football Club and as the national football stadium.

Glasgow has almost 100 cinemas. A Hogmanay fire at the Glen Cinema leads to a stampede, killing sixty-nine children.

Collapse of a stand at Ibrox (Glasgow Rangers) kills twenty. Barmaids are banned by local magistrates.

Kelvin Hall opens to the public.

No Mean City: A Story of the Glasgow Slums is published. Overcrowding in an estimated 29 per cent of households. The subway system goes electric.

Celtic becomes the first British team to win the European Cup, the first 'non-Latin' team to win the European Cup, the first team to win the European Cup with home-grown players, and the first team to win every competition entered in one year (including the BBC's *Quiz Ball*).

Wartime bombing of Clydebank kills 500 people.

Empire Exhibition in Bellahouston Park.

Peter Manuel, convicted of seven murders and later confessing to three more, is hanged in Barlinnie Prison.

Livingston is built to accommodate yet more Glasgow overspill. The last tram runs on 4 September. St Andrew's Halls destroyed by fire.

1938	1941	1958	1962	1967
1939	1956	1960	1966	

Cumbernauld is built to take more Glasgow overspill.

Formation of Upper Clyde Shipbuilders (UCS) from John Brown; Connell, Fairfield; and Stephen and Yarrow.

Cosmo Cinema built (later becoming the Glasgow Film Theatre, still open today).

Cheapside Street whisky warehouse fire kills nineteen firemen.

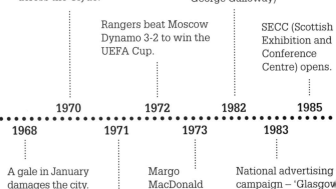

Kingston Bridge takes the M8 traffic across the Clyde.

Rangers beat Moscow Dynamo 3-2 to win the UEFA Cup.

Roy Jenkins wins Hillhead by-election for the new Social Democratic Party (and later loses it to George Galloway)

SECC (Scottish Exhibition and Conference Centre) opens.

1970   **1972**   **1982**   **1985**

1968   **1971**   **1973**   **1983**

A gale in January damages the city. James Watt Street furniture-factory blaze kills twenty people.

Margo MacDonald (SNP) is elected MP for Govan.

National advertising campaign – 'Glasgow Miles Better'. Better than what? Better th anywhere else, bette than you can imagine better than it was, b just better! And to p it, HM The Queen op the purpose-built Bu Collection in Pollok Country Park.

A second Ibrox Stadium disaster kills 66 and injures 145. Erskine Bridge opens. A gas explosion at Clarkston kills twenty. British Government refuses to save Upper Clyde Shipbuilders, leading to the famous 'work-in'.

Opening of new £38 million Clyde Auditorium ('the Armadillo') at the Scottish Exhibition & Conference Centre.

Failed terrorist attack at Glasgow Airport. Glasgow wins the bid for the 2014 Commonwealth Games.

Glasgow is Cultural Capital of Europe, a year-long festival of over 3,000 events. Glasgow Royal Concert Hall opens and the McLellan Galleries re-open. The *QE2*'s return to the Clyde marks fifty years of Cunard.

Celtic are beaten by Porto at the UEFA Cup final in Seville, but win UEFA and FIFA fair-play awards and praise for the supporters' behaviour.

1990	1997	2003	2007
1988	1996	2001	2004

The Garden Festival attracts over 4 million visitors.

Stockline Plastics factory explosion – nine dead, thirty-seven injured.

Gallery of Modern Art opens in the former Stirling's Library. A four-year Festival of Architecture and Design starts, beginning with the first Glasgow Festival of Visual Arts and a large Charles Rennie Mackintosh-retrospective exhibition.

Population falls to around 600,000.

Mysteries and Ghosts

In the 1880s, auctioneer David Dick left his office one afternoon and was met by the ghost of his father, who walked along Renfield Street with him having a chat.

A family who moved into a house in up-market Blythswood Square saw an apparition of a woman drowning a man in the bath. They moved out.

At Barlinnie Prison, near the now bricked-up entrance to the execution block, a ghostly woman in Victorian dress and with a lantern appears.

Before its refit, the Museum of Transport had reports of spooky happenings, such as sightings of a headless woman, ghostly children screaming and balls of blue light coruscating through the place at night.

Glasgow Royal Infirmary is home to a number of entities, including an apparently legless ward sister floating about, and an elderly man (known as Archie) who haunts Ward 27 and talks to dying patients.

O'Brien's Bar in Saltmarket used to receive ghostly visits from an old woman in a shawl – many staff and customers have seen her.

Reston Mather, one of the last owners of Blochairn House in Auchinlea Park, is said to haunt the place.

Staff working in Studio Three at Radio Clyde speak of an unusually aggressive gremlin who not only causes technical glitches but who actually scratched a guest.

The Theatre Royal is haunted by Nora, a young actress who got booed off the stage at an audition and took her own life in shame and despair.

But by far the most famous is the vampire with iron teeth at the Southern Necropolis in the Gorbals – reports in the 1950s said he had caught and eaten two local children, so hundreds more children promptly went looking for him – and even reported sightings to the police. (It was in a horror comic of the time.)

Climate

Glaswegians will tell you that the city has two seasons – July and Raining. Let's be honest – Glasgow is about as far north as Moscow, so what do you expect? But the westerly position and closeness to the prevailing winds and major weather systems of the Atlantic and the Gulf Stream make the climate oceanic, and one of Scotland's mildest. It rarely suffers from the biting winds and 'haar' that mark Edinburgh.

Spring is mild, and the many parks and gardens erupt in a blaze of floral colour.

Summer is unpredictable – either mild and wet or warm and sunny, and sometimes both in one day more than once. The local joke is 'if you don't like the weather, wait 20 minutes'.

Autumns are cool, mild and damp but there is often an unseasonably fine October.

The winters are chilly and damp (the local word is 'dreich'), with leaden skies and temperatures occasionally below freezing. A dry day is rare, but there is hardly ever any snow that lies for more than a day in the city centre. If it does, all traffic grinds to halt and the newspapers predict the end of civilisation.

Annual daytime temperatures: high 19°C/66°F, low 6°C/43°F

Average daily temperature, January: 6°C/43°F

Average daily temperature, June: 17°C/63°F

Annual rainfall: 44ins

Global warming is likely to make Glasgow Britain's wettest city, overtaking Swansea. Another league win!

A Day in Your Life in Glasgow

0609 – First train arrives at Glasgow Central station, from Kilmarnock.

0800 – Have breakfast outdoors in John Street, the city's Italian heart, and maybe window-shop for some Armani.

0830 – Watch the rush-hour from the overpass at The Mitchell.

0900 – Visit the Gallery of Modern Art in Royal Exchange Square to see the works, get free WiFi and marvel that it used to be somebody's house! Check if Wellington is wearing his usual traffic cone.

0945 – Buy coffee and an Empire Biscuit, and people-watch in George Square while munching away.

1000 – Take a hop-on/hop-off bus tour and get to know Glasgow.

1130 – Pop into Kelvingrove Museum and see the Dali.

1230 – Explore the top of Byres Road and have a stroll in the Botanics.

1300 – Enjoy 'a play, a pie and a pint' at the Oran Mor (and see the multi-lingual welcomes and goodbyes).

1400 – Do some gentle shopping at Princes Square and Buchanan Galleries.

1500 – Take afternoon tea in the Rennie Mackintosh-inspired Willow Tea Rooms on Sauchiehall Street.

1600 – Catch an early show at The Stand Comedy Club in Woodlands.

1800 – Have a free trial swim at the beautiful Victorian baths in Arlington Street (ladies Tuesdays, men Wednesdays).

1930 – Dinner at one of the many great restaurants in Ashton Lane, Merchant City or the Pakistani Café in Partick Cross (with literary chat, a bring-your-own-music policy and halal fry-ups).

2030 – Quick pint in The Horseshoe, Drury Street – said to be Europe's longest bar and boasting Karaoke 'eight nights a week'.

2100 – Head for King Tut's Wah Wah Hut on St Vincent Street, where Oasis and local band Glasvegas were discovered. Or for a more intimate venue, try the Captain's Rest on Great Western Road.

2300 – Get cultured at a late-night screening of art-house, cult or classic movies at the Glasgow Film Theatre in Rose Street.

0015 – Last train leaves Glasgow Central station for Ayr.

0100 – Hit the Sub Club, deep below No. 22 Jamaica Street, with possibly the best sound system and DJs in Scotland.

0635 – Take the Glasgow Subway Challenge (get off at Buchanan Street and race the train downhill to board it again at St Enoch).

Glasgow in Numbers

Glasgow's cultural sector employs 3,484 people and brings in £185 million.

1.3 million people annually take in a play or concert, 1 million visit a performance arena, almost 1 million attend festivals and similar events, 3.5 million go to museums, and 4.5 million library visits are made per year (but only 3 million borrowings).

There are over eighty classical orchestral performances each year, with 90,000 attendances (48,000 of these to the RSNO).

King Tut's Wah Wah Hut had 322 performances in 2008-2009, seen by over 85,000 people – but the 160 gigs at the O_2 ABC, O_2 Academy and Barrowlands together attracted more than 350,000.

There are 15,000 cinema seats and 65 screens within Glasgow and almost twice as many in the surrounding area. Sadly, the much-loved Odeon is no more.

Cinemas had 3.5 million attendances, with another 3 million at outer Glasgow venues.

A Glasgow Glossary

Don't laugh, but the bus company now has so many Polish, Slovakian, Czech and Hungarian bus drivers that it has had to teach them the Glasgow 'patter' so they can understand the passengers. 'Professor' Stanley Baxter was famous for his renditions of 'Parliamo Glewsca'. Here are some examples of the local *lingua franca*:

Baltic – rather cold weather for the season, don't you agree?

Bamstick – unintelligent person.

Blootered – slightly the worse for drink.

Braw – splendid.

Buckfast Commando – intoxicated, aggressive and intrepid individual.

Chib – knife, usually not for culinary purposes.

China – friend or colleague (China plate = mate).

Cooncil's built the pavement too near yir bum – you are rather short.

Galloot – ungainly person.

Gallus – worthy of praise.

Gaunnay no dae that – kindly desist.

Gemme's a bogie – there is little point in continuing this endeavour.

Glasgow Kiss – approximation of one's forehead to the nose of an interlocutor (*aka* 'nut cutlet' or 'seborrhea sandwich').

Gutted – disconsolate beyond all telling.

Guttered – see 'Blootered'.

Haud yer wheesht – pray silence.

Havers – conversation devoid of informational value (see Mince).

High Heidjin – person in authority.

Jay think ahm Carnegie? – I cannot afford this item/service/loan.

Kerry oot – off–license sales for later consumption .

Malkey – murder, as in 'Set phasers tae Malkey'.

Mince – something worthless, as in 'Yer talkin' mince!'

Mink – someone of unattractive mien, possibly also a Jakey.

Nyaff – an ungracious person.

Shilpit – of less than appealing physique.

Soapdodger – of inadequate personal hygiene.

Stoater – attractive, especially of young females, or a good goal.

Swally – cocktails, of an evening.

Tongs! – no-one has any idea what this signifies, but it's everywhere.

Wean – a child, or someone who behaves as one, leading to the jibe 'Act yir age, no' yir hat-size'.

Whitsyurgemme? – please explain your actions.

Yabyootay! – this person/thing/event/happenstance is agreeable to me.

Ya Bass! – a general term of approbation.

Yererseisootrawindae – there is scant chance of success in this venture.

Yer Granny! – I find that statement hard to believe (*cf* Havers, Mince).

Glasgow on the Page

'Stiff-necked Glasgow beggar! I've heard he's prayed for my soul,
But he couldn't lie if you paid him, and he'd starve before he stole.'
Rudyard Kipling

'The trouble with Freud is that he never had to play the old Glasgow Empire on a Saturday night after Rangers and Celtic had both lost.'
Ken Dodd

'I would welcome the end of Braid Scots and Gaelic, our culture, our history, our nationhood under the heels of a Chinese army of occupation if it could cleanse the Glasgow slums, give a surety of food and play, the elementary right of every human being, to those people of the abyss.'
Lewis Gibbon, in his polemical essay 'Glasgow'

'Glasgow, the sort of industrial city where most people live nowadays but nobody imagines living.'
Alasdair Gray, _Lanark: A Life in Four Books_

'The great thing about Glasgow is that if there's a nuclear attack it'll look exactly the same afterwards.'
Billy Connolly

'Glasgow is null,
Its suburbs shadows
And the Clyde a cloud.
Dundee is dust
And Aberdeen a shell.
But Edinburgh is a mad god's dream,
Fitful and dark…'
C.M. Grieve (before he became Hugh MacDiarmid),
first published in _Northern Numbers_ No.2,1921

'I may have been born in Calcutta but I was conceived in Glasgow.'
Hamish Imlach

'To me Glasgow is a beautiful warm mess of a city.'
Denise Mina

Famous for...

The warm welcome – Glasgow people are open, funny and generous (when they like you), in contradistinction to Edinburgh's alleged 'You'll have had your tea' attitude (whether they like you or not).

Style – Glasgow is the self-proclaimed capital of the stylish and goes out of its way to prove it in a manner that's hard to dislike.

Proximity to Loch Lomond and the Highlands – The Trossachs are literally 30 minutes from the city centre.

The Glasgow Subway System – The third-oldest underground metro in the world after the London and Budapest versions, Glasgow subway is the UK's only completely underground metro system. The 'Clockwork Orange' nickname is hardly ever used by locals, largely because the old orange livery of the trains has been gradually changed to what's jokingly called 'Blood and Custard' (a nightmare of cream-yellow and carmine).

Education – The excellent universities, medical, dental and veterinary schools, the art achool and education generally.

Bud Neill – In Woodlands Road there is a tribute to this cartoonist and his famous cartoon creations: Lobey Dosser, El Fideldo and Rank Bajin, the resident villain.

The 'Statue of Liberty' – Atop the portico of the Council Chambers, this statue is actually a representation of Truth, but closely resembles the much larger version that appeared off New York two years earlier.

The Glasgow Coma Scale (GCS) – Used all over the world to assess consciousness after head injury and other trauma.

Tourism – Glasgow is one of Britain's most visited cities: over 3 million tourists flock to the city each year.

Infamous for...

Neds – Identifiable by Burberry caps tipped upwards, white tracksuit bottoms tucked into white socks ('budgies') and white fake-designer trainers.

Train delays at Queen Street Station – Irritatingly frequent.

Religious bigotry (on both sides) – This is tied into football, and, to be fair, the clubs themselves try to counteract it.

Orange walks – During the Marching Season, and those who feel it appropriate to shout IRA songs in the streets late at night.

Orange-looking girls – These girls are infamous for wearing 'pelmets' (short skirt and low top) and teetering in heels down city-centre streets on cold nights without coats or apparent discomfort.

Traffic – There is no doubt that the motorway system carved though the heart of Glasgow saved the city from congestion, but it still clogs up at peak times.

One-way systems – People have been known to grow old trying to drive out of Garnethill.

Stretch limos – Choking the streets while taking over-excited teens to hen-night parties.

Seagulls – They can untie bin-bags (it seems) and intimidate anyone carrying something tasty-looking. But, as with the equally-annoying pigeons, Glasgow Council has no statutory powers to deal with them. Glasgow's answer to birds roosting on lamp-posts is to put fake birds on lamp-posts.

Out-of-centre high-rise housing schemes – These were built in the 1960s, and many are now due to come down. Hardly better are the new 'luxury riverside apartments' with 'spectacular views' on the southern bank of the Clyde.

Beggars – Glasgow is infamous for East-European accordion-wielding street beggars, who all seem to know the opening bars of 'La Vie en Rose' and not much else.

Buildings and Architecture

Glasgow is the finest Victorian city in Britain and has architecture considered among the best in Europe. The most impressive buildings include **William Young's City Chambers** in George Square, built at the high point of the 'Second City of the Empire' period.

Around the city are unique examples of work by Glasgow's most renowned architect and designer, Charles Rennie Mackintosh (including the famous **Glasgow School of Art**), and of the equally gifted Alexander 'Greek' Thomson.

Glasgow Central is the second busiest railway station in Britain outside London, after Birmingham New Street, with over 38 million people using it each year – 104,000 per day.

It services five train operators. Opened in 1879 and extended between 1901 and 1906, the fabulous ornate ironwork and pillars won two major station awards in 2009.

Glasgow is a feast for the eyes of lovers of architecture, from the Georgian elegance of **Park Circus** to Art Deco, from the Gothic revival charms of the **Ramshorn church** to the stunning modernity of the **Armadillo** at the SECC and lots of new, confident landmark buildings.

Places to See

The Lighthouse – A stunning building, once a newspaper office.

Glasgow Necropolis – The Père-la-Chaise or Highgate Cemetery of Glasgow, although it outstrips both of these in ornate imagery thanks to merchants who sought to outdo each other posthumously with tombs styled on the countries where they traded.

The grim countenance of John Knox stares down from a high column (though he isn't buried there) and it's tempting to imagine his disapproving frown is due to the ecumenical spirit of the place – the first burial there was Jewish.

St Mungo's Museum of Religious Life and Art – Despite its medieval appearance, this was built in the 1990s.

City Chambers – Fabulous Victorian civic triumphalism.

Kibble Palace Glasshouse – Botanic Gardens.

Buck's Head Building – Designed by Greek Thomson, Buck's Head Building can be found on Argyle Street.

Glasgow Green is home to:

People's Palace and Winter Garden – Declared 'open to the people for ever and ever' by the Earl of Rosebery in 1898.

Doulton Fountain – Donated by Sir Henry Doulton for the Empire Exhibition of 1888, this is the world's largest terracotta fountain.

Templeton's Carpet Factory – Inspired by the Doge's Palace in Venice. Axminster carpets were woven for the *Titanic* here.

McLennan Arch – This arch, if nothing else, has staying power, as this re-modelled Adam brothers' structure was rescued from the demolished Assembly Rooms in Ingram Street and re-sited twice.

Bridges

That Squinty Bridge

Access to Pacific Quay is either by Bell's Bridge (a footbridge) or the Clyde Arc, which goes at an angle across the river – thus falling prey to the Glaswegian delight in frustrating the city fathers by re-naming things whatever they like.

'Squinty Bridge' is far better, as is the story that it was bought second hand from a much wider river, and so had to go at an angle. This was reinforced (if that's the word) when some of the elastic snapped about sixteen months after its official opening on 18 September 2006. A spokesman at the time said 'We don't believe the integrity of the bridge is affected… [it] is designed to allow for the removal of one of the bridge supports at a time… without affecting its operation', which of course meant it had to be shut for nearly six months until 28 June 2008. Now it's back to its usual 6,500 crossings a day.

Here is the full list of the twenty-one bridges over the Clyde, and construction dates of their latest incarnations:

Dalmarnock Bridge, 1891

First Dalmarnock Railway Bridge, 1861

Second Dalmarnock Railway Bridge, 1897

Rutherglen Bridge, 1896

Polmadie Bridge, 1955

King's Bridge, 1933

St Andrew's Suspension Bridge, 1856

Pipe Bridge and Weir, 1901

Albert Bridge, 1871

The City Union Railway Bridge, 1899

Victoria Bridge, 1854

South Portland Street Suspension Bridge, 1853

Glasgow (Jamaica Street) Bridge, 1899

First Caledonian Railway Bridge, 1878

Second Caledonian Railway Bridge, 1905

George the Fifth Bridge, 1928

Tradeston Footbridge, 2009

Kingston Bridge, 1970

Clyde Arc, 2006

Bell's Bridge, 1988

Millennium Bridge, 2002

Museums

Glasgow's museums reflect its various cultural influences. Here's a selection of the best:

Glasgow Police Museum – Not the official one at Pitt Street but the much better volunteer version in Bell Street. The ex-polis guides have a tendency to grip you firmly by the elbow as they take you round!

The world famous Burrell Collection in the prize-winning **Pollock Country Park** – A purpose-built gallery opened in 1984 to house the unconventional and anarchic artefacts gifted to Glasgow by the ardent (if unfocused) collector Sir William Burrell.

The magnificent **Glasgow Art Gallery and Museum** in Kelvingrove – Houses the city's principal collection of paintings and has Scotland's most frequently visited free attraction: Dali's 'Christ of St John of the Cross'.

The Transport Museum or Riverside Museum – Glasgow Trams, locomotives, an exact reconstruction of old Glasgow streets, and (possibly) the world's oldest bicycle.

St Mungo's Museum of Religious Life and Art – Opposite and reflecting Provand's Lordship, Glasgow's oldest building still in use.

Royal Highland Fusiliers Museum in Sauchiehall Street – everything a regimental museum should be, in a shop-front.

Glasgow Gallery of Modern Art (GoMA) – A brand-new gallery set in the refurbished Stirling's Library and housing the city's principal post-war art collection.

Scotland Street School – A Charles Rennie Mackintosh building now preserved as Glasgow's Museum of Education.

The People's Palace – The true collective memory of Glasgow's economic, social and political past from the residents' perspective.

How many visitors annually?

Museum/Gallery	Visitors
Kelvingrove	1,368,000
GOMA	537,000
Museum of Transport	469,000
People's Palace	269,000
Burrell	203,000
St Mungo's	144,000
Provand's Lordship	117,000
Pollok House	86,000
Hunterian Art Gallery	80,000
Hunterian Museum	79,000
Scotland Street School	65,000
Scottish Football Museum	41,000
Tall Ships Museum	29,000
Glasgow School of Art	25,000
Royal Highlands Fusiliers	3,000
Riverside Museum incorporating the Museum of Transport (new)	500,000 in its first 2 months

A Glasgow First?

Is this the world's oldest bicycle?

Gavin Dalzell certainly thought it was when he displayed his model at the 1888 Glasgow International Exhibition.

But the honour may go to another Scot, Kirkpatrick MacMillan, whose 1840 invention may predate Dalzell's by a few years. On the other hand, the French will tell you the father-and-son team of Pierre and Ernest Michaux invented it – but not until 1861.

The World's Oldest Bicycle ... Or is it?

Parks and Green Spaces

Glasgow takes the 'dear green place' epithet seriously, and there are over ninety parks and open spaces – more than in any other city Glasgow's size.

The five listed historic gardens and designed landscapes are:

The **Botanic Gardens** with the exotic Kibble Palace.

Kelvingrove Park, with one of the Europe's best collections of bronze statues.

The Glasgow Necropolis, behind the High Church.

Pollock Park, with its Highland cattle and Clydesdale horses. Voted 'Britain's Best Park' in 2007 by the Royal Horticultural Society and 'Europe's Best Park' in 2008 by Briggs and Stratton. It is Glasgow's largest park and also houses the Burrell Collection. Pollock Park also has Pollock House and the renowned Stirling Maxwell collection of Goya, Blake, El Greco and more.

Victoria Park has the Fossil Grove, a fascinating display of eleven fossilised tree trunks more than 300 million years old, part of the carboniferous forest which became the coal seams to power Glasgow's industry.

Others:

Glasgow Green is the oldest public park. It contains the stone on which James Watt is said to have sat, thinking up the inventions which sparked the Industrial Revolution.

Queen's Park with Scottish Poet's Rose Garden and fabulous views.

Bellahouston Park, site of the Empire Exhibition of 1938.

Tollcross Park, venue for the annual International Rose Trials, a children's zoo and an international sports centre with a 50-metre pool.

Scientists and Inventors

Joseph Black taught both chemistry and medicine at Glasgow in the eighteenth century and gave us our modern understanding of gases.

James Watt conducted some of his early experiments with steam power while working at Glasgow University.

Adam Smith, economist and philosopher, started as a student at Glasgow when he was fourteen. In 1751 he returned as Professor of Logic, transferring to the Chair of Moral Philosophy shortly afterwards. He had left the university by the time his most famous work, *The Wealth of Nations*, was published, but later returned as rector.

Dr Joseph Lister, working in the Glasgow Royal Infirmary, was the first to sterilise surgical equipment.

Lord Kelvin, the founding father of modern physics, was born William Thompson in Belfast in 1824. The family relocated to Glasgow when he was nine. He studied at Glasgow University and returned at the age of twenty-two to the chair of natural philosophy (physics), which he held for fifty-three years. Kelvin had an international reputation for his experiments and established the Kelvin temperature scale (absolute zero at -273.15°C).

John Logie Baird was busy trying to create diamonds by heating graphite when he shorted out the entire electrical supply for Glasgow! Born in nearby Helensburgh in 1888, his studies at the two universities were interrupted by the First World War and never resumed. But he did invent television with the first transmission of an image in 1924 and improved colour television in 1928.

John Boyd Orr (Baron Boyd Orr of Brechin) campaigned for an adequate diet for the people during the First World War and Depression and continuing through the rationing of the next war. His food plan produced a better nourished population and he received the Nobel Peace Prize for his work with the United Nations.

Ian Donald, professor of midwifery at the Glasgow University, pioneered the use of ultrasound scanning using technology from the shipbuilding industry to detect flaws in metal.

The world's best selling muscle relaxant, Atracurium, was designed and synthesised by a University of Strathclyde team led by **John Stenlake**, based on South-American use of curare to paralyse blow-dart victims.

Sir James W. Black won the Nobel Prize for his groundbreaking work on beta-blockers and the control of gastric acid production which revolutionised stomach ulcer therapy. Born in Uddingston, he worked at Glasgow Veterinary School in the 1950s.

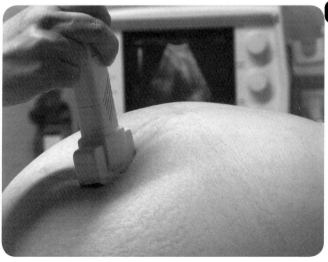

Explorers and Adventurers

Sir Arthur Whitten Brown – Navigated the first successful non-stop flight across the Atlantic Ocean with Sir John William Alcock as pilot, beating Charles Lindbergh by eight years. The flight, in a modified Vickers Vimy bomber, from St John's, Newfoundland, to Clifden, Connemara, Ireland, took 16 hours and 12 minutes on 14 June 1919 and won the £10,000 prize offered by the *Daily Mail*.

James Allan Mollison – A pioneer aviator who set a number of records during the 1920s and '30s, including being the youngest officer in the Royal Air Force (at eighteen), the youngest ever instructor at Central Flying School (at twenty-two) and the shortest flights from Australia to England in 1931 (8 days, 19 hours) and England to South Africa in 1932 (4 days, 17 hours).

David Livingstone – What more can be said about the great doctor-missionary-explorer of Africa? He studied both medicine and theology at what was then Anderson's University. His statue dominates the plaza in front of Glasgow High Church.

Musicians

Adam McNaughton – Folk singer (famous for the Jeely Piece song)

Alex Harvey – Rock singer (Sensational Alex Harvey Band)

Amy McDonald – Singer

Archie Fisher – Scottish folk singer

B.A. Robertson – Songwriter and producer

Bert Jansch – Guitarist (died 2011, aged sixty-seven)

Billy Boyd – Actor and musician (Beefcake)

Brian Robertson – Guitarist (Thin Lizzy)

Cilla Fisher – Singer and performer (The Singing Kettle)

Clare Grogan – Singer and actress (Bill Forsyth's film *Gregory's Girl*)

Donovan – Early folk-pop legend

Eddi Reader – Singer (Fairground Attraction)

Frankie Miller – Soul singer, songwriter and actor ('McAfferty, yer tea's oot!')

Hamish Imlach – Influential folk performer

Hamish Stuart – Guitarist/vocalist (Average White Band)

Iain Mackintosh – Folk singer

Jack Bruce – Influential bass player (Cream)

Jim Diamond – Singer-songwriter and producer

Jimmy Somerville – Singer and gay icon
(Bronski Beat, Communards)

John Martyn – Singer-songwriter and guitarist brought up
in Shawlands

Lena Martell – Cabaret and gospel singer, born Helen Thomson

Lonnie Donegan – Skiffle legend

Lulu – Entertainer and 1960s icon, born Marie Lawrie

Maggie Bell – Rock and blues singer

Maggie Reilly – Singer, collaborator with Mike Oldfield

Malcolm and Angus Young – Rockers, founding members
of AC/DC

Mark Knopfler – Singer and guitarist (Dire Straits)

Matt McGinn – Folk singer, poet and 'Two-Heided Man'

Midge Ure – Musician (Thin Lizzy, Rich Kids, Visage, Ultravox)

Onnie McIntyre – Musician (Average White Band)

Stuart MacMillan, Slam-DJ and co-producer of the Soma
record label

Bands

Altered Images – Early 1980s post punk band

Aztec Camera – Roddy Frame's band, debut album 1983

Beatstalkers – Scotland's number one beat band in the 1960s

Beefcake – Winner of the Tartan Clef Best Live Act 2008

Belle and Sebastian – Wistful indie seven-piece band

Blue Nile – Formed in 1981 by Glasgow University graduates

Bluebells – 1980s band, founded by Robert Hodgens

Camera Obscura – Indie pop band created in 1996

Deacon Blue – A band fronted by Ricky Ross

Del Amitri – Met at school in Glasgow in 1980

Delgados – Indie band named after a Tour de France winner

Franz Ferdinand – Post punk revival band set up in 2002

Fratellis – Name possibly inspired by *The Goonies*

Glasvegas – Indie rock band formed by the Allan cousins in 2003

Hipsway – Started by ex-Altered Images bassist Jon Mcelhone

Hue and Cry – Formed by the Kane brothers in 1983

JSD Band – Celtic folk group who started on the folk club circuit

Love and Money – First came together in 1985

Mogwai – Named after creatures from the film *Gremlins*

Primal Scream – Became popular after 1991 album *Screamadelica*

Silencers – Celtic rock band formed in 1986

Simple Minds – Best known for song 'Don't You (Forget About Me)'

Skyscraper Wean – Named after 'The Jeelie Piece Song'

Texas – First performed at the University of Dundee in 1986

Travis – Inspired by a character from the film *Paris, Texas*

Performing Arts Organisations

Scottish Opera – Scotland's National Opera Co. is the largest performing arts organisation in Scotland. Founded by Sir Alexander Gibson, in 1974 it purchased the Theatre Royal and reopened it as Scotland's first national opera house. The Orchestra of Scottish Opera followed in 1980.

Scottish Ballet – The national dance company for Scotland was founded by Peter Darrell and Elizabeth West as Western Theatre Ballet in Bristol in 1957 but moved to Glasgow in 1969. In 2009 the company moved to new purpose-built national headquarters at the Tramway International Arts Centre.

Royal Scottish National Orchestra – No question, this is one of Europe's leading symphony orchestras. Originally a freelance orchestra brought together to accompany performances by the Glasgow Choral Union, under the guidance of Sir Alexander Gibson it became the Scottish National Orchestra in 1950, becoming Royal in 1991.

BBC Scottish Symphony Orchestra – Brought together in 1935 by Scottish composer-conductor Ian Whyte, this leading UK orchestra has a busy broadcasting schedule on BBC radio and television and also records commercially. It has won many awards, including the Royal Philharmonic Society and Gramophone.

National Youth Orchestras of Scotland – Notice the plural 'orchestras', because this unique organisation boasts eight ensembles, in classical, jazz and contemporary music, for students aged eight to twenty-five.

Citizen's Theatre – The iconic venue and theatre company in the Gorbals first opened as a theatre in 1878, but the Citizens Co. was founded in 1943 by James Bridie, and the theatre permanently established in 1945. Since then it has become one of Scotland's premier producing theatres.

Actors and Comedians

Alex Norton – Actor (*Taggart*)

Bill Paterson – Actor (*Comfort and Joy*, *Gregory's Girl* and *Miss Potter*)

Billy Boyd – Actor (*Lord of the Rings*)

Billy Connolly – Comedian, actor and ranter

Craig Ferguson – Actor, comedian and US chat-show host (*The Late Late Show with Craig Ferguson*)

David Hayman – Actor (*Trial and Retribution*)

David McCallum – Television and movie star (*Man from Uncle* and *NCIS*)

David O'Hara – Actor (*Braveheart*, *The Devil's Own* and *Hotel Rwanda*)

Donald Meek (1878-1946) – Actor in over 100 Hollywood films

Dorothy Paul – Comedienne, actor and national treasure (*The Steamie*)

Duncan Macrae – Actor (*Para Handy*, *Casino Royale*, 1967)

Elaine C. Smith – Comic actor (*Rab C. Nesbitt*)

Ford Kiernan – Comic actor (*Chewing the Fat* and *Still Game*)

Frankie Boyle – Cutting-edge comedian

Gary Lewis – Actor (*Gangs of New York*, *Rebus* and *Billy Elliot*)

Gerard James Butler – Law graduate, actor and singer (*300*)

Gerard Kelly – Actor and panto favourite (*City Litghts*, *Rab C. Nesbit* and *Scotch and Wry*)

Gordon Jackson – Actor (*Upstairs, Downstairs* and *The Professionals*)

Greg Hemphill – Comic actor (*Chewing the Fat* and *Still Game*)

Gregor Fisher – Comedian, actor (*Love Actually* and *Rab C. Nesbitt*) **Ian and Jeanette Tough** – Better known as The Krankies.

Ian Richardson – Actor (*House of Cards*) **Jack Milroy** – Comedian (part of double act Francie and Josie) and panto actor

James McAvoy – Actor (*The Last King of Scotland*)

Jane McCarry – Comic actor (*Still Game*)

Jimmy Logan – Comedian and entertainer

John Barrowman – Actor and game-show host (*Dr Who* and *Torchwood*)

Molly Weir – Much-loved actress (*Rentaghost*)

Paul Riley – Comic actor (*Still Game*)

Ray Park – Stuntman and martial artist (*Star Wars*)

Rikki Fulton – Comedian (part of double act Francie and Josie) and comic actor (*Late Call*)

Robbie Coltrane – Actor (*Cracker* and *Harry Potter*)

Robert Carlyle – Renowned actor (*Trainspotting*)

Sir Jeremy Isaacs – Television producer, BAFTA and Emmy-award winner

Stanley Baxter – Comic actor and entertainer

Tommy Flanagan – Actor (*Braveheart* and *Gladiator*)

Among the luminaries who trod the boards at the Panopticon in the Trongate – the oldest surviving music hall in Britain, dating back to 1857 – were Dan Leno, Harry Lauder, Marie Loftus, Jack Buchanan and, making his debut in 1906, the sixteen-year-old Stan Laurel. His father managed the Metropole theatre, and his mother, actress Margaret Metcalfe Jefferson, is buried in Glasgow's Cathcart cemetery.

The 1,500-strong Panopticon audience enjoyed the reputation that 'no turn was left unstoned'.

Glasgow in Film

Glasgow has its own Film Office within the Council to promote the city as a filming location.

Star Wars

There is no connection here, except that Glaswegian actor Ray Park played Darth Maul in *Star Wars Episode I: The Phantom Menace*. To make up for the obvious lack of attention, Glaswegians have a long tradition of jokes about exactly why the *Star Wars* movies weren't made in Glasgow, including:

R2D2 would be mistaken for a bin and everyone would try to stuff chip papers into his head;

Fluent in over 3,500 languages, C3P0 would still not understand anything said to him in the East End;

Obi-Wan Kenobi would be addressed as 'Big Yin';

The Millennium Falcon would have tinted windscreens, a saltire bumper sticker and a *Daily Record* 'I Love Scotland' sticker in the back window;

The best way to destroy the Death Star would be to leave it parked and unattended in Easterhouse.

However, here are some **real** movies made in Glasgow:

Legacy
Glasgow became New York for this psychological thriller shot in 2009 starring Idris Elba.

Red Road and Donkeys
The first two parts of the Advance Party trilogy were shot in 2006 and 2008 respectively.

Shallow Grave
Danny Boyle's 1994 black comedy, starring those unknowns Ewan McGregor and Christopher Eccleston alongside old-stagers Peter Mullan and Ken (Rebus) Stott, was mainly shot in Glasgow, apart from the necessary Edinburgh exteriors. Not to give the plot away, the body was buried in Rouken Glen and the car was dumped at Mugdock Country Park.

Trainspotting
Likewise, director Boyle largely filmed Irvine Welsh's Edinburgh-set novel in Glasgow, notably the old Wills' Cigarette Factory on Alexandra Parade, and the famous Begbie pint-glass-off-a-balcony episode was shot in Crosslands, Queen Margaret Drive, which now has an oil painting of the scene in the upstairs seating area of the pub. The movie is in the British Film Institute's top ten British films of all time.

World War Z
Brad and Angelina were all over town – and so were about a zillion zombies! Glasgow city centre became Philadelphia's financial district for a couple of weeks in July 2011 and 2,000 Glaswegian extras got to lurch about, moaning and looking ghastly. Locals said it was no different from a normal Saturday night in George Square.

Novelists and Writers

James Kelman – Booker Prize winner, 1994.

Christopher Brookmyre – Winner of the First Blood Award for best first crime novel of the year.

Karen Campbell – *The Twilight Time* and *After the Fire*.

Alasdair Gray – Scottish writer and artist. Best known for his novel *Lanark*, published in 1981.

Clifford Hanley – Journalist and novelist best remembered for his novel *Dancing in the Streets*.

James Kelman – Wins many plaudits for his novels, stories, plays and political essays including, controversially, the 1994 Booker Prize (for a novel written in working-class Glasgow dialect) and in 2008 Scotland's most prominent literary award, the Saltire Society's Book of the Year.

Tom Weir MBE – Author, broadcaster and climber, member of the first post-war Himalayan expedition in 1950 and best known for his long-running television series *Weir's Way* and trademark woollen bunnet.

Denise Mina – Scottish crime writer, known for her Garnethill trilogy and a further three novels featuring the Glasgow journalist Patricia Meehan, but also a comic-book writer (thirteen issues of *John Constantine – Hellblazer* for DC) and author of two plays.

Archie Hind – Author of award-winning novel *Dear Green Place*.

Louise Welsh – Her 2002 debut novel *The Cutting Room* was nominated for a number of literary awards, including the Orange Prize for Fiction, and won the Crime Writers' Association Creasey Dagger for the best first crime novel.

Chris Dolan – The award-winning poet, author and playwright writes regularly for radio and screen, and his screenplay for his novel *An Anarchist's Story* was broadcast by the BBC in 2006.

John McGlade – He has worked on Channel 4's *Clive Anderson Talks Back*, ITV's *The Baldyman* and several BBC Scotland Comedy Unit productions.

Grant Morrison – comic book writer (*New X-Men, The Invisibles, Animal Man* etc).

Poets

A.C. Clarke – Makar for the Federation of Writers in Scotland from 2007-8.

Ivor Cutler – Eccentric poet, songwriter and humorist, who died in 2006.

Fleming Carswell – Retired medical scientist, notable for having poems published in less traditional places such as *The Lancet*.

Lesley Duncan – Poetry editor of *The Herald* and its daily poem, was co-editor of *The Edinburgh Book of Twentieth-Century Scottish Poetry*.

Graham Fulton – Well-known for his poetry performances. Works include *Die Michael Palin, Die*.

Magi Gibson – Held Royal Literary Fund and Scottish Arts Council Fellowships and won the Scotland on Sunday/ Women 2000 Prize.

Iyad Hayatleh – Palestinian poet resident in the city since 2000, Iyad is a member of Artists in Exile, Glasgow.

Irene Hossack – Her collection, *North of All Borders*, contains a series of poems on Glasgow.

A.B. Jackson – Won the third Edwin Morgan International Poetry Competition in 2010 with his poem 'Treasure Island'.

David Kinloch – Founding editor of *Verse* magazine, and is currently reader in English at the University of Strathclyde.

Frank Kuppner – Has been Writer in Residence at the Universities of Glasgow and Strathclyde. His *A Bad Day for the Sung Dynasty* won the Scottish Arts Council book award in 1984.

THE OBSCURE HISTORY OF THE MERCHANT CITY:
c.1820 FORMERLY 183, THE HOUSE OF STEPHEN
MILLER WHO WAS THE WONDERFUL WEAN OF
THE POEM OF THAT NAME, BY HIS FATHER,
WILLIAM MILLER, AUTHOR OF THE FAMOUS
WEE WILLIE WINKIE. 1851 HOUSE OF THOMAS
WYLDE OF THE MANUFACTURING FIRM ROGER
WYLDE AND SON. 1957 JOHN PLAYER AND SONS
OFFICE DEVELOPMENT FOR THEIR BRANCH OF
THE IMPERIAL TOBACCO COMPANY.

151
GEORGE STREET
MERCHANT CITY

GLASGOW CITY COUNCIL
MERCHANT CITY TOWNSCAPE HERITAGE INITIATIVE

Liz Lochhead – Much-honoured poet, playwright and artist, who was made Glasgow's Poet Laureate in February 2005 and is now Makar (national poet).

Alan MacGillivray – Chosen for the Scottish Poetry Library's anthology Best Scottish Poems in 2009.

Edwin Morgan OBE – Scotland's first Makar and winner of the Queen's Gold Award for poetry, in 2010 he left £1 million in his will to the Scottish National Party to help the cause of independence.

Michael Munro – Poet and lexicographer who has also written books on lexicography, including the Glasgow dialect.

Nalini Paul – Came to Glasgow via India and Vancouver and in 2011 was the George Mackay Brown Writing Fellow in Orkney.

Alan Riach – Professor of Scottish Literature at Glasgow University, he has published four books of poetry.

Michael Schmidt OBE – Born in Mexico, studied at Harvard and Oxford and is currently Professor of Poetry at Glasgow University. Honoured for services to poetry in 2006.

Hamish Whyte – Runs the poetry publisher Mariscat Press and has edited numerous anthologies including *Mungo's Tongue's: Glasgow Poems 1630-1990*.

Two of Glasgow's almost-forgotten poets are fortunately memorialised on building and street plaques: **Thomas Campbell** (1777-1844) and **Stephen Miller** (1810-1872), who wrote *Wee Willie Winkie*. Campbell's house is next to the Old College bar in the High Street, which claims to be Glasgow's oldest pub.

Glasgow – Media City

Glasgow is the headquarters for Scotland's main media organisations. The main newspapers include:

Daily Record – Known to its detractors as *The Daily Rangers*, the *Daily Record* is a tabloid newspaper. Formerly Scotland's best-selling daily paper (307,794 copies in August 2011), the *Daily Record* is now outstripped by arch-rival the *Scottish Sun* (circulation of almost 340,000 in Scotland in September 2010).

The Sunday Mail – This is the weekend version of the *Daily Record*, with the same left-wing perspective and read by over a million people each week, making it the biggest selling Sunday paper in Scotland – much to the fury of the Tory-leaning *Daily Mail*, which had to name its Sabbath incarnation *Mail on Sunday*.

The Herald – With an audited circulation of 47,226 in August 2011, it beats Scotland's other 'quality' national daily, the Edinburgh-based *Scotsman*.

Evening Times – The evening sister-paper of *The Herald*, the *Evening Times* was established in 1876 and claims 'Nobody Knows Glasgow Better'. The old 1868 *Times* and *Herald* building (by Rennie Mackintosh) in Mitchell Street is now the Lighthouse, the Centre for Architecture, Design and the City.

Sunday Post – A Scottish institution, but now dated in outlook, this paper was launched by DC Thomson in 1914, and its rather sentimental and nostalgic feel gave it the highest per-head readership of any publication in the world at one time (Guinness Book of Records), now declining from 700,000 in 1999 to around 330,000.

There are also Scottish editions of English newspapers:

Scottish Daily Express
Scottish Daily Mail
Scottish Mirror
Sunday Times Scotland
The Scottish Sun
The Times

Broadcast Media

Glasgow is the headquarters of:

BBC Scotland (TV and radio) since 1923, and now out of the old Queen Margaret Drive building, to the dismay of its largely West End-resident staff.

STV, Scottish Television, the local ITV franchise.

Real Radio, located in nearby Ballieston, the pop music, news and football station is the most listened to station in Scotland.

Radio Clyde in nearby Clydebank, an independent radio station covering the Greater Glasgow area.

Capital FM, formerly Beat 106 and Galaxy, is part of a nine-station UK hit music network.

Quite possibly the greatest newspaper headline ever (right), after Inverness Caledonian Thistle trounced UEFA Cup semi-finalists Celtic 3-1 in February 2000. (You have to sing it to the *Mary Poppins*' tune...)

SUPER CALEY
GO BALLISTIC
CELTIC ARE
ATROCIOUS

Barnes dragged into the gutter

ELEVEN days ago the guttering on the Lisbon Lions Stand collapsed — last night it was John Barnes' badly-built TEAM that came crashing down around his ears.

Make no mistake, Steve Paterson's men will go down in history — Barnes and his side will go down in infamy.

If it was the most glorious night in Super Caley's six-year League history, it was also the blackest evening in the 112 years of once mighty Celtic.

They were surpassed, outfought and outwitted by a team expected to be little more than cannon fodder.

The Parkhead faithful looked on in disbelief as their megabucks idols were played off the park.

As the Highlanders went to their 3,000 fans to kick off the party at all Scottish Cup parties, the remaining Celtic supporters gaped in astonishment at the scenes of sheer joy.

Nightmare

They could only have been praying to wake up from the bigger nightmare of their lives.

Then the ones who could summon

and Berkovic set up two chances the first for Yiduka who slid past the post and the second cracked off a post by Stephane Mahe.

A Wieghorst shot was saved by Cal-der and when Yiduka pounced on the rebound the big Aussie saw his effort blocked by defender Stuart Golabek.

There was controversy when Valgaeren was eventually sent off.

When Berkovic and Burchill teamed up again the striker's shot slammed off Calder and the chance was gone.

Desperate

Rab Kinnier brought down Wilson from behind and Sheerin showed why he has played 91 consecutive games by easily slotting the ball past Gould to put Celtic in desperate trouble.

FINCH ME ... a disbelieving Marc McCulloch dives on goal hero Wilson

CELTIC ..... 1 INVERNESS CT 3
By Rodger Baillie at Parkhead

Journalists and Broadcasters

Andrew Marr – Ubiquitous television and radio presenter, and political pundit, Marr was born in Glasgow in 1959.

Gavin Esler – Presenter of BBC 2's *Newsnight*, BBC World arts and culture programme *Hardtalk Extra* and BBC Radio 4 foreign affairs series *Four Corners*, Esler was also previously BBC Washington Correspondent. He was born in Glasgow in 1953.

Harry Benson – The multi award-winning photojournalist has had a sixty-year career based in America but, by his own admission, firmly based in his Glasgow roots. He got to the USA at the same time as the Beatles, has photographed every American president since Eisenhower, was there when Richard Nixon resigned and just feet away from Bobby Kennedy when he was killed. Many of his photographs have iconic status.

Kirsty Young – Born in 1968 in East Kilbride but educated in Stirling, Young is the main presenter of *Crimewatch* and *Desert Island Discs*. Married to millionaire nightclub-owner Nick Jones, she was presenter of the main evening news programme for Scottish Television from 1992 and also hosted her own chat show. Kirsty then joined the news team of the new Channel 5 in 1997, leaving in 1999 but returning in 2002.

Lorraine Kelly – A television presenter, journalist and actress, Kelly was born in 1959 in Glasgow. She turned down a place at university to study English and Russian when offered a job on the *East Kilbride News*, and later joined BBC Scotland as a researcher, moving to an on-screen role as Scottish reporter for TV-am in 1984. Among other activities, she is agony aunt for *RAF News*.

Kirsty Wark – One half of the Wark-Clements production company (with husband Alan, but no longer involved since the take-over by the Zodiak Media Group), Wark was born in Dumfries in 1955 and educated in Ayrshire and Edinburgh, but is now firmly Glasgow-based. She is best known for presenting BBC 2's *Newsnight* (since 1993) and the weekly arts segment *The Review Show.*

Lord Reith – Although born in Stonehaven in 1889, Reith was educated in Glasgow and his first job was as an apprentice engineer with the North British Locomotive Co. there. Running the BBC from 1922 to 1938, he set the high standards for the broadcaster in his deeply-held Presbyterian values, but clashed with both Winston Churchill and Labour leaders over their political views – he was an admirer of both Hitler and Mussolini before 1939.

Janice Forsyth – Now best known as a radio presenter (*The Janice Forsyth Show* and *The Radio Café*), she has been a central character in the Glasgow arts and media scene for years, since graduating from Glasgow University in english literature and drama. She was a key player in Mayfest before moving to work in newspapers, TV and radio.

Pacific Quay

The former **Plantation Quay and Princes' Dock** Basin (the largest on the Clyde when it opened in 1900 until its demise in the 1970s, thanks to containers) was the site for the Glasgow Garden Festival in 1988. It then struggled to find a role, but it now houses a number of activities.

The **4 Winds Pavilion**, which had been a pumping house and generating station to power the electric cranes, is now home to a consultant engineering company and to Capital FM Scotland.

This sits alongside **Glasgow Science Centre and IMAX**, plus **Glasgow (or Millennium) Tower**. This 'antenna spire' stands 127 metres tall and is the tallest free-standing structure in Scotland as well as the highest tower in the world capable of rotating 360 degrees – at least, in theory. The 65cm diameter bearing is not connected to the foundations but sits in a 15-metre deep socket and is shaped like a big aircraft wing jammed into the ground so that it faces into the wind. However, a raft of safety and engineering problems, notably with the rotating bearing, meant it was closed from February 2002 to August 2004, and on 30 January 2005, ten people spent five hours trapped in the lifts, so it shut again for another two years.

Occasionally nutters abseil from it – and why do they bother, as Glasgow Tower has two lifts and 523 stairs? (But this is not the first tower on the site – the **Clydesdale Bank Tower** stood on more or less the same spot during the Garden Festival.) Next door is **BBC Scotland**'s unlovely and unloved headquarters and studios, variously known as 'PQ' or 'the box the Science Centre came in'. The STV building next door is known as 'the box the plug came in'.

Glasgow School of Art has a Digital Design Studio for research and commercial work.

One of the **Rotundas** – originally these two circular brick buildings were elevators at either end of the Glasgow Harbour Tunnel from Tunnel Street to Plantation Place. Built between 1890-96, at the height of Glasgow's tunnelling mania, there were three parallel tunnels – one for pedestrians (closed on 4 April 1980) and two for horses and carts – with a hydraulic lift at each end. The North Rotunda is currently a casino, but the South Rotunda sits unused – amazing, as the whole Pacific Quay area has not a single pub or restaurant to service all those BBC, STV and other workers on site.

Business Then...

Sir William Burrell – The shipping magnate and philanthropist amassed an eclectic collection. Quite what possessed him to bring a wall from Hornby Castle, Yorkshire, is beyond knowing. His collection is now in Pollock Park.

James McGill – Businessman and philanthropist who founded McGill University in Canada after emigrating there in 1766 to work in the fur trade. A plaque in Stockwell Street commemorates his birthplace.

Sir Thomas Lipton – Creator of the famous Lipton tea brand and famous for his advertising stunts, such as putting gold coins in a cheese just before Christmas – causing such panic buying that the police had to step in.

Miss (Kate) Cranston – Entrepreneur, developer of a successful chain of tea rooms and major patron of our famous architect and designer Charles Rennie MacKintosh and his wife Margaret MacDonald.

Clyde Ships – Over 22,000 vessels were built by Clyde Ships, including the *Queen Mary*.

Locomotive Construction – a quarter of all the world's trains were built in Glasgow at one time, until the decline of the 1960s. Much of this was located in Springburn, with the North British Locomotive Co., the Saracen Foundry and Charles Tennant's engineering works. Now, part of the St Rollox railway works is a maintenance facility, and the maintenance depot for the Glasgow Subway system.

Business Now...

Glasgow has the UK's third-highest GDP per head (after London and Edinburgh) with over 400,000 jobs in 12,000 companies. Between 2000 and 2005, a staggering 150,000 jobs were created.

Govan's legacy of shipbuilding and engineering remains in **BAE Systems Surface Ships** shipyards and precision engineering **Thales Optronics**.

There are still major manufacturing firms in Glasgow: **Aggreko**, **Albion Motors**, **British Polar Engines**, **Clyde Blowers**, **Firebrand Games**, **Howden**, **Linn HiFi**, **Weir Group**, and in the food and drink sector, **Edrington Group**, **Whyte and Mackay** and **William Grant**.

Lord Macfarlane of Bearsden – Entrepreneur and founder of the Macfarlane Group, who also ran the fund-raising campaign for the refurbishment of Kelvingrove.

The Weir Group started in 1871 as a pump manufacturer and the Weir double-acting steam pump was standard on most British-built steamships as late as the 1950s. In 2007 the Glasgow-based Weir Pumps was sold to Jim McColl (another Glasgow entrepreneur and Scotland's richest man, according to the *Sunday Times*), becoming Clyde Pumps Ltd.

Michelle Mone OBE (opposite) – The Ultimo Bras supremo is regarded as one of Scotland's top entrepreneurs. She courted controversy in 2010 by posing in her own lingerie ads, but who better, frankly?

MGB Biopharma is developing a new antibiotic to treat the deadly MRSA and *Clostridium difficile* bugs, based on DNA minor groove binding technology licensed from the University of Strathclyde.

R.S. McColl, purveyors of all thing sweetie-ish and newspapery, was started by 'Toffee Bob', better known as the Robert Smyth McColl, who played for Queen's Park, Newcastle and Rangers and won thirteen Scotland caps.

Political Figures

Sir Henry Campbell-Bannerman – Leader of the Liberal Party from 1899 to 1908 and Prime Minister of the UK from 1905 to 1908, but born Henry Campbell in 1836 at Kelvinside House in Glasgow.

Andrew Bonar Law – Prime Minister of the UK from 1922-23 and Unionist (Conservative) MP for Glasgow Central from 1918-23.

Gordon Brown – Prime Minister of the UK 2007-10 and MP for Kirkcaldy, where he grew up, although he was born in Glasgow in 1951.

Donald Dewar – Former Secretary of State for Scotland, First Minister of Scotland when the Scottish Parliament was reconvened in 1999 and a Labour MP in Glasgow from 1978 to his death in 2000. His statue by Kenny Mackay stands in front of the Royal Concert Hall in Buchanan Street, Glasgow – occasionally seen wearing a tartan scarf and bunnet in the cold weather, thanks to some well-meaning soul.

Sir Menzies Campbell – Former leader of the Liberal Democrats (2006 to 2007) and MP for North East Fife, but born and educated in Glasgow. 'Ming' was captain of the Great Britain athletics team in 1965 and 1966 and held the British 100 metres sprint record from 1967 to 1974 (10.2 seconds).

Sir John A. MacDonald – Canada's first Prime Minister was born somewhere in or near the Merchant City in 1815 but his father's debts from an unsuccessful business drove the family to emigrate when John was five. There is a plaque commemorating him on the Ramshorn church, but no statue in Glasgow.

Michael Martin – The first Scottish Speaker in the House of Commons and the first Catholic to hold that office since the Reformation, Labour MP for Glasgow Springburn from 1979 to 2005, then for Glasgow North East until 2009, Speaker of the House of Commons from 2000 to 2009 and subsequently created Baron Martin of Springburn.

Jimmy Reid – Trade Union activist, orator, politician, journalist.

Bashir Maan – Britain's first Muslim local councillor, elected in Glasgow in 1970.

George Nicoll Barnes – Leader of the Labour Party from 1910-1911 and a Glasgow MP from 1906-1922.

Roy Jenkins – A founder of the SDP and the MP for Glasgow Hillhead (1982-1987), having served as president of the European Commission from 1977-1981 (the only Briton to occupy that position).

The Tobacco Barons

The Tobacco Lords (or Virginia Dons) were Glasgow merchants who, in the eighteenth century, made enormous fortunes by trading in tobacco from Great Britain's colonies. A number had grand mansions which gave their names to Glasgow streets, including:

Alexander Oswald

Andrew Buchanan

Andrew Cochrane

Archibald Ingram

James Dunlop

James Wilson

John Glassford

The Virginia Mansion of Alexander Speirs gave the name of Virginia Street and Speirs Wharf in Port Dundas, Glasgow.

And it's fame of a sort having your name on a pub window some 200 years after your death.

Freedom of the City

The Freedom of the City is the greatest tribute Glasgow can offer any person and is conferred by the Lord Provost of Glasgow to 'persons of distinction or persons who have rendered eminent service to the City'.

Historically, Freemen and Burgesses have the same rights and privileges: the right to graze their cows on the common land (Glasgow Green), the right to fish on the Clyde, the duty to patrol and guard the town (watch and ward), the duty to defend the town by arms (failure to do so carrying a charge of perjury), and the right to a prison cell of their own (that is, without un-Freemen in it).

Freemen do not have to associate with un-Freemen. They have the duty to pay the equivalent of today's valuation tax and the right to be present at all court hearings.

The Freedom of the City has been bestowed on:

Aung San Suu Kyi

Benno Schotz

Billy Connolly

Harry McShane

Jim Watt

Kennie Dalglish

Lord MacFarlane

Nelson Mandela

Sir Alex Ferguson

Sir Samuel Curran

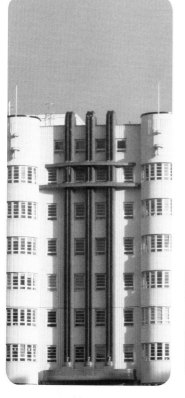

The Hyndland Bear

Stop at the traffic lights at the top of Crow Road facing the shops at Hyndland and you'll see Glasgow's most famous teddy bear.

Always dressed appropriately for the weather (duffel coat and wellies or Hawaiian shirt and sunglasses) or in the strip of the football team playing at home that week, the Hyndland Bear receives postcards from his friends worldwide and displays them in the window of his first-floor flat.

Surely a candidate for Freedom of the City?

Fictional Characters

Scrooge McDuck – Disney's 'richest duck in the world' is uncle to Donald Duck and great-uncle to Huey, Duey and Luey.

Groundskeeper Willie – The Simpsons' character is allegedly from Glasgow, but his red hair and equally fiery temper betray a Highland origin.

But far and away the most famous Glasgow literary characters are the **detectives**:

Dick Donovan – Nationally and internationally popular before Sherlock Holmes, Dick Donovan, the Glasgow Detective, was conceived by novelist and journalist J.E.P. Muddock, initially while working for DC Thomson in Dundee.

Allan Pinkerton – Created the first detective agency in the USA (the Pinkerton Agency – famous for its private-eye logo). He was real, but his life and exploits have become fictionalised over time. For example: he was NOT born in a house that is now the site of a Glasgow mosque; his father was NOT the first police sergeant, who was NOT killed or injured in a riot; he did NOT get married in a hurry and escape the next day to avoid capture for 'Chartist' political activity; and he did NOT organise the killing of the Jesse James Gang (Pinkerton had been dead two years by 1886).

Taggart – To the cry of 'There's been a murder', a body in a raincoat gets dragged out of the Clyde regularly on this long-running police drama series, which is so popular that not even the death of the actor playing the eponymous hero (Mark McManus) has halted its run.

Sporting Figures

Sir Alex Ferguson – Football legend and manager of Manchester United.

Alex McLeish – Scotland footballer and manager, who took Rangers to two championships and five cups in five years.

Alison Sheppard MBE – Freestyle swimmer who has competed in five consecutive Olympics from 1988 and was Female World Cup Overall Winner 2002-2003.

Andy Murray – Scotland's highest ranked tennis player and world number two in 2009. Yet the Wimbledon title continues to elude him, probably due to confused – or sardonic – fans shouting 'Come on, Tim!'

Arthur Graham – Footballer for Aberdeen, Leeds United, Manchester United, Bradford City and Scotland, mainly as a left-winger, and now involved with the Leeds United Academy.

Benny Lynch – Scotland's first boxing champion, holder of the British, European and world flyweight titles in the 1930s.

Danny McGrain – Footballing legend, selected for Celtic's all-time greatest eleven and now assistant coach of the club's development squad.

Gerry Hughes – Teacher, and the first deaf yachtsman to cross the Atlantic (2005), Hughes is planning a single-handed round-the-world non-stop attempt for 2012.

Glasgow Mid-Argyll – The 1973 Camanachd winning team at shinty, a Highland game related to Irish hurling and older than recorded history.

Jim Watt – World lightweight champion 1979, who retired with a record thirty-eight wins (twenty-seven by knockout) and eight losses and is now a boxing commentator.

John Wark – Footballer, mostly for Ipswich Town, who won twenty-nine caps and scored seven goals for Scotland, and appeared in the film *Escape to Victory* with Sylvester Stallone.

Kenny Dalglish – Footballer for Celtic and manager of Liverpool.

Members of the 1972 UEFA Cup Winners Cup team (Rangers FC): Alex MacDonald and Willie Johnston.

Members of The Lisbon Lions (Celtic FC), winners of the European Cup (to date, the only Scottish team to do so): Ronnie Simpson, Jim Craig, Bobby Murdoch, Stevie Chalmers and Bertie Auld.

Mo Johnston – Footballer, and the second player ever to have played for both Rangers and Celtic since the Second World War (the first being Alfie Conn).

Paul Weir – Two-time World Champion boxer and undefeated WBO Minimum Weight Champion.

Tommy Docherty – Footballer and manager of various teams, including Scotland.

Sports

Fitba' Crazy

Love of football is endemic in Glasgow. The world's first international football match was held in 1872 at the West of Scotland Cricket Club in the Partick area of the city (a 0–0 draw between Scotland and England).

Glasgow is one of only three cities with two football teams in European finals in the same season (Liverpool and Madrid are the others). In 1967 Celtic won the European Cup final and Rangers were in the Cup Winners' Cup final.

The Glasgow Cup, at one time a tournament between **Celtic**, **Clyde**, **Partick Thistle**, **Queen's Park** and **Rangers**, now involves the youth sides of the same five teams.

Rangers were so named after an English Rugby Union club in 1872 but are also known as the Gers, Teddy Bears or Light Blues. They are not officially called Glasgow Rangers. They play at the 51,082-seat Ibrox Stadium and have more top national championships than any other club in the world, including fifty-four League Championships. They hit near-terminal financial troubles in 2012.

Other Sports

Much of Glasgow's life is tied up with sport, and the city gloried in the titles UK National City of Sport 1996-99 and European Capital of Sport 2003. The **Kelvin Hall International Sports Arena** is the venue for a number of sporting events.

State-of-the-art sports facilities in Glasgow include these world-class football grounds: the new **National Stadium,** Hampden Park, which includes the **Scottish Football Museum**; **Ibrox Stadium**, the home of Rangers Football Club; **Celtic Park**, which has been recently refurbished; and **Scotstoun Stadium**, which, after an £18 million redevelopment, now has facilities that include a 400-metre athletics track, a 25-metre swimming pool, rugby pitches and the National Badminton Academy.

Major Sporting Events

The **Great Scottish Run** is the third biggest race in the UK of its type and the largest participation sports event in Scotland, attracting over 20,000 entries in 2011.

UEFA Champions League Cup Final in May 2003 was watched by an estimated 400 million people worldwide.

The **Special Olympics National Summer Games** took place in 2005, involving some 1,500 athletes with learning disabilities competing in athletics, sailing, golf, equestrian, swimming, judo and other sports.

And, of course, everyone is looking forward to the **Commonwealth Games** in 2014 – Glaswegians call the London 2012 Olympics 'the rehearsal' – and there is considerable building work and regeneration around the East End as the stadium and other sporting facilities are built.

One of the main reasons Glasgow won the bid for the 2014 Games was having over seventy of the venues already in place, and all close to the planned Athletes Village in Dalmarnock. However, there will be a new 5,000-capacity National Indoor Sports Arena and Velodrome in Parkhead, opposite Celtic Park.

Picture Credits

unless otherwise stated, pictures are either by Carolyn Becket or Bruce Durie, or not in need of a credit.

128